ABOUT TH

Peter Nichols spent bankrupt after his King's Road theme restaurant, de Sade's, was raided by vice squad officers investigating complaints about his novel way of force-feeding black puddings and pineapples to his customers. He now works for a leading firm of estate agents, putting up For Sale boards.

Harvey Jones has written articles for *Vogue*, *Tatler*, and *Harpers & Queen* (none of which have been published) but this is his first attempt at serious journalism. He lives in a studio flat in North-West Knightsbridge borders (i.e. Acton). He recently paid £2000 for an 071 telephone number.

OTHER JOINT PUBLICATIONS BY PETER NICHOLS & HARVEY JONES

Your Disgrace: The Correct Etiquette on How to Address a Duke's Bastard

the KNIGHTSBRIDGE GIRL
joke book

Peter Nichols and Harvey Jones

CORGI BOOKS

THE KNIGHTSBRIDGE GIRL JOKE BOOK
A CORGI BOOK 0 552 13974 2

First publication in Great Britain

PRINTING HISTORY
Corgi edition published 1992

Copyright © Peter Nichols and Harvey Jones 1992

The right of Peter Nichols and Harvey Jones to be identified as authors of this work has been asserted in accordance with sections 77 and 78 of the Copyright Designs and Patents Act 1988.

Conditions of sale

1. This book is sold subject to the condition that it shall not, by way of trade *or otherwise*, be lent, re-sold, hired out or otherwise circulated in any form of binding or cover other than that in which it is published *and without a similar condition including this condition being imposed on the subsequent purchaser.*

2. This book is sold subject to the Standard Conditions of Sale of Net Books and may not be re-sold in the UK below the net price fixed by the publishers for the book.

This book is set in 12/14pt Plantin

Corgi Books are published by Transworld Publishers Ltd, 61–63 Uxbridge Road, Ealing, London W5 5SA, in Australia by Transworld Publishers (Australia) Pty Ltd, 15–23 Helles Avenue, Moorebank, NSW 2170, and in New Zealand by Transworld Publishers (NZ) Ltd, 3 William Pickering Drive, Albany, Auckland.

Printed and bound in Great Britain by
Cox & Wyman Ltd, Reading, Berks.

the KNIGHTSBRIDGE GIRL
joke book

DEDICATION

To all the girls who made
it possible

FOREWORD

This remarkable volume is a welcome addition to Corgi's Tribes of Britain series, which also includes Ray Leigh and Brent Wood's seminal study of Essex Girls.

Like their eastern counterparts, Knightsbridge Girls have been with us for generations. In fact, the interbreeding which has taken place in this insular community helps explain why they all look alike.

Their close-knit world revolves around shopping, riding and skiing. Lacking the intelligence of their Essex sisters, they tend to be employed by their fathers in undemanding positions in art galleries, interior decoration, public relations and, of course, publishing.

Peter Nichols and Harvey Jones have conducted minutes of painstaking research into the customs, habits and mores of this fascinating species and produced a revealing social document. As they say in Knightsbridge: 'Get your gums round this, gel.'

Sir Beauchamp Place
Knightsbridge Scatological Institute
1992

What do Knightsbridge Girls use that's six inches long and buzzes?

A. A mobile telephone.

What's the perfect birthday gift for a Knightsbridge Girl?

A. Saddle soap-on-a-rope.

Why does a Knightsbridge Girl have a retriever?

A. To stop her man from getting away.

Why is a Knightsbridge Girl like the TSB?

A. They both want to know how much money you have before they say 'yes'.

Why did the Knightsbridge Girl turn down a holiday in Holland?

A. One simply never goes Dutch.

What's big and pink and too hard for a Knightsbridge Girl in the morning?

A. The *Financial Times*.

What does a Knightsbridge Girl use instead of a telephone directory?

A. *Who's Who*.

Knightsbridge Girl goes into a chemist's shop: 'I'd like some deodorant.'
  'Aerosol?'
  'No. It's for under one's arms.'

Why do Knightsbridge Girls buy their boyfriends loose boxer shorts?

A. They just adore coming-out balls.

Why do Knightsbridge Girls have babies?

A. To give the red setter something to play with.

Knightsbridge Girl to Hooray Henry: 'Would one like sex?'
   Hooray Henry: 'Top hole!'
   Knightsbridge Girl: 'Later. Remember one's manners. Tits first.'

How do you make a Knightsbridge Girl smile?

A. Shove a coathanger in her mouth.

What is a Knightsbridge Girl's idea of primal therapy?

A. Watching a nanny eat chocolate biscuits.

Why do Knightsbridge Girls have children?

A. It pushes up the alimony settlement.

What do Knightsbridge Girls make for dinner?

A. Reservations.

What does a Knightsbridge Girl do after having sex in the countryside?

A. Mucks out the stable.

A pregnant Knightsbridge Girl asked her doctor in which position she should give birth.

'The same position as the one in which you conceived the baby.'

'What? In the back seat of Jeremy's BMW?'

What's a Knightsbridge Girl's favourite Beach Boys song?

A. Barbour Ann.

How do Knightsbridge Girls find out the time?

A. They slam the Golf door and wait till someone yells: 'Shut up, don't you know it's four o'clock in the morning?'

What positions do Knightsbridge Girls make love in?

A. 'POSITIONS?'

What does a Knightsbridge Girl call her boss?

A. Daddy.

What's the difference between a Knightsbridge Girl and the Rolling Stones?

A. The Rolling Stones thought you *can't* always get what you want.

What's the similarity between a Knightsbridge Girl and a slice of processed cheese?

A. They both get eaten in Rolls.

What's a Knightsbridge Girl's favourite
Joe Orton play?

A. *Loot*.

What's a Knightsbridge Girl's second
favourite Joe Orton play?

A. *Entertaining Mr Sloane*.

What's the difference between a
Knightsbridge Girl and a donkey?

A. One brays and looks like a horse and
the other's a donkey.

What's the only difference between
Knightsbridge Girls and Labradors?

A. Labradors are loyal.

What's the difference between a Knightsbridge Girl and Jeremy Beadle?

A. At least Jeremy Beadle smiles after he's shafted someone.

What do you call a car accident in Knightsbridge?

A. A crèche.

What's the difference between dancing with a Knightsbridge Girl and being tackled by Vinny Jones?

A. You're less likely to get bruised ankles with Vinny Jones.

What do Knightsbridge Girls say on their wedding night?

A. 'You *can* lose it riding, you know.'

Why is a Knightsbridge Girl like Pimms No 1?

A. They both get drunk at garden parties.

What's the difference between Knightsbridge and Greenland?

A. There aren't so many Huskies in Greenland.

Why does a Knightsbridge Girl drink champagne at parties?

A. As a pick-me-up.

Knightsbridge Girl is taken to the National Gallery. Her boyfriend says: 'Oh, look. There's Whistler's Mother.'

'Didn't we meet her at the Hunt Ball?'

What's the difference between a Knightsbridge Girl and the Abominable Snowman?

A. One likes Alpine conditions and is hideously ugly to look at and the other is also known as a Yeti.

What's the difference between a Knightsbridge Girl's son and Richie Havens?

A. Richie Havens only *sometimes* feels like a motherless child.

What's the difference between a Knightsbridge Girl and her mother?

A. One looks like a fifty-year-old hag and the other one's her mother.

What's the difference between a Knightsbridge Girl and a goldfish?

A. A goldfish is more interesting when it opens its mouth.

What does a Knightsbridge Girl say when she reaches an orgasm?

A. 'I'm arriving, I'm arriving!'

What's the difference between a Knightsbridge Girl and the moon?

A. The moon doesn't apply foundation to its pockmarked surface.

Why do Knightsbridge Girls make love with the light off?

A. Because one can't bear to see one's chap having a spiffing time.

Why is a Knightsbridge Girl like a travelling rug?

A. They both get laid on picnics.

Knightsbridge Girl to Knightsbridge Boy: 'Would you like to go dine on me tonight?'
   'Yes please. If you're paying we'll go to the Savoy.'

What's the difference between a
Knightsbridge Girl and a snowman?

A. You get more warmth from a snowman.

What's the difference between
Knightsbridge Girl and Chelsea Girl?

A. One's noisy and has hundreds of frocks
and the other's a boutique.

What do you call a Knightsbridge Girl
with an 'O' Level?

A. The Princess of Wales.

What do you call a Knightsbridge Girl
with two 'O' Levels?

A. Unique.

What's the similarity between a Knightsbridge Girl and the Brazilian rain forest?

A. They're both pretty dense.

What's the difference between a Knightsbridge Girl and the Brazilian rain forest?

A. The Brazilian rain forest is rapidly becoming less dense.

Where do Knightsbridge Girls have their country houses?

A. Bray.

What did the polo player do when he was bored with the Knightsbridge Girl?

A. Chukka.

What do randy Knightsbridge Girls say to the man they fancy?

A. 'Would one like to give one one?'

What do you call a Knightsbridge Girl in a city boardroom?

A. The caterer.

How do you tickle a Knightsbridge Girl?

A. Gucci, Gucci, goo.

What's a Knightsbridge Girl's idea of natural childbirth?

A. Absolutely no make-up.

What's the difference between a Knightsbridge Girl and a pig?

A. One's greedy and squeals and the other's a pig.

What's the difference between putting your hand inside a Knightsbridge Girl's bra and driving a Skoda?

A. You feel a bigger tit in a Skoda.

Why did the Knightsbridge Girl get banned from Vidal Sassoon?

A. She kept drinking the shampoo.

What's the difference between the coastline of Britain and a Knightsbridge Girl's bum?

A. The Knightsbridge Girl's bum isn't getting any smaller.

What is a Knightsbridge Girl's favourite pop group?

A. Bucks Fizz.

What does a Knightsbridge Girl use for protection during sex?

A. A Purdey.

Why did the Knightsbridge Girl refuse to move South of the River?

A. She considered Clapham Common.

Why is eating out with a Knightsbridge Girl like committing a crime?

A. Crime never pays, either.

What's the difference between a bottle of beer and a Knightsbridge Girl?

A. You have to take the top off a bottle of beer before it will satisfy you.

What do a Knightsbridge Girl and Vick's Synex have in common?

A. Both get up your nostrils.

What's the difference between a Knightsbridge Girl and Vick's Synex?

A. You feel ill *before* you come into contact with Vick's Synex.

What's the difference between a Knightsbridge Girl and Sandhurst?

A. Fewer officers have been through Sandhurst.

What do you call a Knightsbridge Girl in Oxford Street?

A. Lost.

What's the difference between a Knightsbridge Girl and a Silver Lady?

A. One gets screwed on the bonnet of Rolls-Royces and the other's a mascot.

How does a Knightsbridge Girl tell her husband that she is going to have their child?

A. 'Darling, we're going to need a nanny.'

Why did the Knightsbridge Girl return the Rolex Oyster she was given as a birthday present?

A. There was no R in the month.

What's the difference between a Knightsbridge Girl and the NatWest Tower?

A. Fewer merchant bankers have been up the NatWest Tower.

Why is a Knightsbridge Girl like a tin of mushrooms?

A. They're both cultivated but have no taste.

What's a Knightsbridge Girl's idea of a blind date?

A. Going out with someone she isn't related to.

What's the difference between a Knightsbridge Girl and a solid wooden table?

A. One's thick and gets laid before lunch and the other's a useful piece of furniture.

Why is a Knightsbridge Girl like Oliver Reed?

A. Because they're both always on the piste.

And then there was the Knightsbridge Girl who trained to be a secretary. On her first day she typed her first letter. On her second day she typed the other 25.

What do you call a group of singing Knightsbridge Girls?

A. A Barbour shop quartet.

What's the similarity between a Knightsbridge Girl and catarrh?

A. They both get up your nose.

What's the difference between a Knightsbridge Girl and catarrh?

A. One's thick and gives you a headache and the other's an accumulation of mucus.

Why do Knightsbridge Girls get married?

A. So they can appear in *Hello!*

What's the difference between a Knightsbridge Girl and the Antarctic?

A. One's cold, uninviting and miles away and the other's a wasteland near the South Pole.

Why did the Knightsbridge Girl opt for a Caesarian birth?

A. She didn't fancy the idea of labour.

What have a Knightsbridge Girl and a dishwasher got in common?

A. They've both got plenty of Finish but only one washes dishes.

What's the only thing cultured about a Knightsbridge Girl?

A. Her pearls.

And then there was the Knightsbridge Girl who thought Pearl Harbor was a discount jeweller's shop in Brompton Road.

How does a Knightsbridge Girl apologize for not having been born in Knightsbridge?

A. 'Surrey.'

What is a Knightsbridge Girl's favourite sexual position?

A. Facing Harrods.

What does a Knightsbridge Girl mean when she says she wants to be kissed somewhere warm, wet and smelly?

A. She wants to be taken to India.

What do you call a Knightsbridge Girl at Cambridge University?

A. Just visiting.

Where do Knightsbridge Girls buy their milk and butter?

A. Jennifer's Dairy.

Why did the Knightsbridge Girl go to the East End?

A. Because she heard that the men would give one a pony if one slept with them.

What's the difference between a Knightsbridge Girl and an orbiting space satellite?

A. The orbiting space satellite is more down to earth.

Why is a Knightsbridge Girl like a roofer?

A. They're both always out on the tiles.

Where do Knightsbridge Girls meet their friends?

A. Whine bars.

What's the difference between a Knightsbridge Girl and a night watchman?

A. A night watchman usually gets out of bed before 6.00 in the evening.

What's the difference between a Knightsbridge Girl and a circus elephant?

A. One has a large nose and gets laughed at for its dancing and the other one's called Dumbo.

Knightsbridge Girl to her friend: 'Shall we go and see the Chippendales?'

'No, I prefer modern furniture actually.'

What does a Knightsbridge Girl like best before SEX?

A. SUS.

What is a Knightsbridge Girl's favourite old record?

A. Last Train to San Lorenzo.

What do you call a Knightsbridge Girl working in a stockbroker's office?

A. The interior decorator.

Knightsbridge Girl goes into a shop and asks for some pepper.

'White pepper or black pepper, modom?' asks the assistant.

'No. Toilet pepper.'

Why is a Knightsbridge Girl like a brassière?

A. They both get on your tits.

Why is a Knightsbridge Girl's fiancé like a Soho gambling club after it's been hit by the Triads?

A. They're both chinless.

What's the difference between a Knightsbridge Girl and a bottle of perfume bought from an illegal trader in Oxford Street?

A. There's more chance of the perfume being genuine.

Why do Knightsbridge Girls think it is safe to smoke?

A. Because duty-free cigarettes don't carry health warnings.

What's a Knightsbridge Girl's biggest dilemma?

A. Half-price Barbours for sale in Kilburn.

Why do art dealers hire Knightsbridge Girls to work in their galleries?

A. So the pictures look great by comparison.

How many Knightsbridge Girls does it take to change a lightbulb?

A. Two. One to open the champagne and the other to phone the electrician chappie.

What's a Knightsbridge Girl's favourite place to go after a hard day's fox-hunting?

A. Blood-U-Like.

What's the difference between a Knightsbridge Girl and a used-car salesman?

A. One is insincere and out to screw you for every penny and the other sells used cars.

What does a Knightsbridge Girl have in common with the statement 'Albania is the richest country in the world?'

A. They're both incredibly false.

What does a Knightsbridge Girl in public relations do?

A. What does anyone in public relations do?

What does a Knightsbridge Girl say during foreplay?

A. 'I take it this means we're engaged, Henry.'

Which two words are emblazoned on every Knightsbridge Girl's heart?

A. Trust Fund.

Why do Knightsbridge Girls walk round with their noses in the air?

A. So they don't have to smell their own breath.

And then there was the particularly stupid Knightsbridge Girl who thought Val d'Isère was an Irish folk singer.

What designer label does a Knightsbridge Girl wear in her knickers?

A. Next.

Why do Knightsbridge Girls wear blue stockings?

A. To hide their varicose veins.

What's the only charming thing about a Knightsbridge Girl?

A. Her bracelet.

What does a Knightsbridge Girl say when her boyfriend gets a stiffie?

A. 'Add it to the others on the mantelpiece.'

And then there was the Knightsbridge Girl who boasted that she was bilingual because she could say 'yes' in German.

What's the similarity between a Knightsbridge Girl and Beluga caviar?

A. You have to be very rich to eat either of them.

What's the difference between a Knightsbridge Girl and Beluga caviar?

A. They both taste of fish but only the caviar gives you satisfaction.

Why is a Knightsbridge Girl like an aircraft carrier?

A. You should give them both a wide berth.

And then there was the Knightsbridge Girl who married a Saudi prince. She became known as the Shriek of Araby.

What's the difference between a Knightsbridge Girl's party smile and a poker game in Dodge City?

A. The poker game is less likely to be fixed.

Why don't Knightsbridge Girls enter beauty contests?

A. Because shopping doesn't count as a hobby.

And then there was the Knightsbridge Girl who thought sex were things you kept coal in.

Why is a Knightsbridge Girl like a Ferrari?

A. They both cost a fortune and are hard to get into.

Why don't Knightsbridge Girls put carrier bags over their heads when they have sex?

A. Why do you think they wear scarves?

What do you call a Knightsbridge Girl's address book?

A. Debrett's.

Why do Knightsbridge Girls eat rich food?

A. To improve their complexions.

What does a Knightsbridge Girl take before sex?

A. Two bottles of Bollinger.

Why are Knightsbridge Girls like snow?

A. They're both thick on the ground in Klosters.

What cup size does a Knightsbridge Girl usually take?

A. Pimms No 1.

Why do Knightsbridge Girls insist on eating goat's cheese?

A. Because Nanny knows best.

What's the difference between a Knightsbridge Girl and the Elephant Man?

A. One is frighteningly ugly and gets the hump if anyone is rude to them and the other one was played by John Hurt.

And then there was the Knightsbridge Girl who caught a burglar in her house. She dialled 999 and screamed 'There's a heist in my hice.'

How can you tell when a Knightsbridge Man is sexually excited?

A. By the stiff upper lip.

Why are Knightsbridge Girls like Cinderella?

A. They have ugly sisters.

What's the difference between a Knightsbridge Girl and Cinderella?

A. No-one would ever dare tell a Knightsbridge Girl she couldn't go to the ball.

What's a Knightsbridge Girl's favourite chat show?

A. *Aspen and Company*.

What's the difference between a
Knightsbridge Girl and a Pushmi-Pullyu?

A. One is two-faced and the other is a
character in a Dr Dolittle book.

Why did the Knightsbridge Girl run out of
ice for the gin and tonics?

A. It was Cook's day off and she'd taken
the recipe with her.

What is a Knightsbridge Girl's idea of
enthusiasm?

A. 'Oh, if you *must*, Rodney.'

Why do Knightsbridge Girls spend so
much money on their flats?

A. Because charity begins at home.

Why does a Knightsbridge Girl get up before 4.00 p.m?

A. So she can get to Coutts before it shuts.

What is a Knightsbridge Girl's idea of sincerity?

A. Falling in love with a man who has less money than she has.

Why is a Knightsbridge Girl like an IBM computer?

A. Because she'll never go down on you.

What's the difference between a Knightsbridge Girl and a coal fire?

A. A coal fire gives out some warmth when you poke it.

What's the similarity between a
Knightsbridge Girl and Johnny Rotten?

A. They're both pretty vacant.

What's the difference between a
Knightsbridge Girl and Johnny Rotten?

A. Johnny Rotten wasn't given a £250,000
ring to change *his* name.

What's the difference between a
Knightsbridge Girl and a Penguin?

A. It only costs a few pence to pick up a
Penguin.

What's the difference between a Knightsbridge Girl and Lassie?

A. One has foul breath and has sex on all fours and the other one makes films with Elizabeth Taylor.

What's the difference between a Knightsbridge Girl and the Mona Lisa?

A. You get a smile from the Mona Lisa.

What's the difference between a Knightsbridge Girl and a St Bernard?

A. One's a dog up a mountain with a bottle of brandy and the other's a St Bernard.

What does a Knightsbridge Girl say after sex?

A. 'Do you all play for the same polo team?'

Why is a Knightsbridge Girl like a boxer?

A. They'd both kill for a title.

What's a Knightsbridge Girl's idea of loyalty?

A. Asking her friend *before* she sleeps with her husband.

How does a Knightsbridge Girl commit a social faux pas?

A. By eating her bread roll instead of throwing it.

What's the difference between a Knightsbridge Girl and a puddle?

A. One is shallow and best avoided and the other one's a puddle.

What's the difference between Dolly Parton and a Knightsbridge Girl?

A. Only Dolly Parton's tits are false.

What's the difference between a Knightsbridge Girl's bedroom and Euston Station?

A. There's never any shortage of Guards in a Knightsbridge Girl's bedroom.

Why do Knightsbridge Girls wear high heels?

A. All the better for looking down on you.

What do you call an intelligent Knightsbridge Girl?

A. Living proof that Mummy slept with the butler.

Who, for Knightsbridge Girls, is the patron saint of dinner parties?

A. St Michael.

Why do Knightsbridge Girls always take a friend with them when they shop for clothes?

A. Because even the shop assistants can't bring themselves to say 'Oh, it really suits you.'

What is the difference between a Knightsbridge Girl and Lord Snooty?

A. Lord Snooty's pals are genuine.

How do you get rid of a Knightsbridge Girl?

A. Tell her you're broke.

Why do Hooray Henrys marry Knightsbridge Girls?

A. So that their children will be more intelligent than them.

What do a Knightsbridge Girl and a diminutive professional jockey have in common?

A. They're both quick to get on their high horse.

What's a Knightsbridge Girl's idea of being flat broke?

A. Being down to her last three apartments.

What's the difference between a Knightsbridge Girl and *Thunderbirds*?

A. *Thunderbirds* is animated and has Brains.

How can you tell when a sick Knightsbridge Girl is getting better?

A. She orders a cocktail cherry in her medicine.

Why do Knightsbridge Girls wear velvet hairbands and pearls?

A. So they don't have to bother telling the cabbie where they want to go.

What do you call a Knightsbridge Girl with a social conscience?

A. A traitor.

What do you call a Knightsbridge Girl who doesn't work for Daddy?

A. Overqualified.

How do you know when a Knightsbridge Girl has had an orgasm?

A. She puts down her copy of *Horse and Hound*.

Why don't Knightsbridge Girls use public transport?

A. 'What's public transport?'

Why did the Knightsbridge Girl visit the monastery?

A. Because she thought she heard they were always going to Klosters.

What do a Knightsbridge Girl and a pimp have in common?

A. They both have more brass than taste.

Why is a Knightsbridge Girl like a soft-boiled egg?

A. They both get soldiers dipped into them.

What do a Knightsbridge Girl and a boy who has bought food at a funfair have in common?

A. They both have a tendency to be toffee-nosed.

What is a Knightsbridge Girl's favourite movie?

A. *Sloane Alone*.

Why do Knightsbridge Girls have facial hair and deep voices?

A. Because they want to be like their mothers.

When a Knightsbridge Girl lost her credit card her husband didn't report it to the police. The thieves didn't spend as much as she did.

Why is a Knightsbridge Girl like a constipated farm-worker?

A. They both have piles in the country.

Why do Knightsbridge Girls get married so young?

A. So they don't have to wait too long for the first alimony payments.

Why do Knightsbridge Girls go on skiing holidays?

A. Because life's not just one long party.

And then there was the Knightsbridge Girl who thought that loose change was when you put on a tracksuit.

What are the only two French words in a Knightsbridge Girl's vocabulary?

A. 'Le' and 'Gavroche'.

What is a young Knightsbridge Girl's favourite cartoon character?

A. Barbour the Elephant.

Why do Knightsbridge Girls wear strapless dresses?

A. They're never strapped for anything.

Why does Harrods's telephone number end in the digits 1234?

A. So Knightsbridge Girls can show off their counting skills.

What's the difference between Rob Andrew and a Knightsbridge Girl?

A. One's a stand-off and the other's stand-offish.

Naval officer to Knightsbridge Girl: 'Have you ever seen HMS *Hermes*?'
　'Isn't that the Queen's headscarf?'

Why do Knightsbridge Girls work in PR?

A. After partying all night it's the only work they're capable of doing.

What is a Knightsbridge Girl's idea of foreplay?

A. 24 hours' unlimited use of a Harrods credit card.

What is a Knightsbridge Girl's favourite Vietnam war movie?

A. *Full Dinner Jacket*.

Why did marriage hold no surprises for the Knightsbridge Girl?

A. Because she'd already slept with a groom.

What's the difference between marriage to a Knightsbridge Girl and a heroin habit?

A. One's very expensive and will eventually drive you mad and the other's illegal.

What is a Knightsbridge Girl's favourite sauce?

A. Daddy's.

What do you call a Knightsbridge Girl with inherited brains?

A. Adopted.

One Knightsbridge Girl to another: 'I don't understand why people are moaning about unemployment.'
    'Me neither, darling. There was a story in the *Daily Mail* today which said there are 50,000 jobs in somewhere called Jeopardy.'

What's a Knightsbridge Girl's idea of a horror movie?

A. *Down and Out in Beverly Hills*.

Why is a Knightsbridge Girl like a lemonade salesman?

A. They both get all their money from Pop.

What birthday present do you give to a Knightsbridge Girl who's studying Zen philosophy?

A. A fur coat.

Why do Knightsbridge schools have such long holidays?

A. So that the children can get to know the new nanny.

Knightsbridge Girl: 'Mummy, where's the television channel changing thingy?'
   'It's thingy's day orf, darling. You'll have to do it yourself.'

Why do Knightsbridge Girls marry their cousins?

A. Because they're not allowed to marry their brothers.

What does a Knightsbridge Girl have in common with John Cleese?

A. They know people who spend all their time being Idle.

What is the difference between a Knightsbridge Girl's father and Arthur Daley?

A. Arthur Daley is only a *minor* villain.

How does a Knightsbridge Girl satisfy the man in her life?

A. She gives him an Essex Girl.

Why does Knightsbridge have a tube station?

A. So that charladies can get to work.

Why did the Knightsbridge Girl have so many middle names?

A. Because Mama, Papa, Step-Mama and Step-Papa all wanted to have their say.

Why does a Knightsbridge Girl announce her engagement in *The Times*?

A. So that Rodney can't back out of it.

What's the difference between a Knightsbridge Girl and Jimmy Hill?

A. Jimmy Hill eventually got round to shaving *his* chin.

Why is a Knightsbridge Girl like a greengrocer?

A. They both speak with plums in their mouths.

Pregnant Knightsbridge Girl is asked by her mother who the father is.
   'How am I supposed to know? You never let me go steady with anyone.'

Why do Knightsbridge Girls believe in God?

A. Well, someone must have built Harrods.

How does a Knightsbridge Girl tell a Knightsbridge Boy it's all over?

A. 'Darling, Daddy's lost all of his money.'

And then there was the Knightsbridge Girl who liked the sound of Franz Liszt because she thought he might be related to Wedding List.

What are the last two letters in the Knightsbridge Girl's alphabet?

A. VW.

What's a Knightsbridge Girl's favourite opera?

A. *The Barbour of Seville*.

Knightsbridge Boy to Knightsbridge Girl: 'Let's play Mummies and Daddies.'
'OK. I'll have the flat and you can keep the place in the country.'

What's the difference between a Knightsbridge Boy and a homosexual?

A. One's into rogering people with moustaches and the other's gay.

Why does a Knightsbridge Girl like the best things in life?

A. Because she likes anything that's free.

What's the difference between a Knightsbridge Girl and a tramp on the Embankment?

A. One's a lazy good-for-nothing who wears ill-fitting clothes and the other one sleeps in a cardboard box.

And then there was the Knightsbridge Girl who thought the Green Belt was something that would go nicely with her wellingtons.

Why does a Knightsbridge Girl snort cocaine?

A. Because one's got to use up one's allowance somehow.

Why does a Knightsbridge Girl close her eyes when she's making love?

A. So she can pretend she's shopping.

How do you know if you've slept with a Knightsbridge Girl?

A. There's a finger-bowl by the bed.

Knightsbridge Girl to Hooray Henry at breakfast: 'No toast, Roger?'
  'Sorry darling. The Queen.'

Why are Knightsbridge Girls put in dormitories at their boarding schools?

A. So that they can bore each other to sleep.

And then there was the Knightsbridge Girl who thought *Play Your Cards Right* was all about hiding the Access bill from Daddy.

Why don't Knightsbridge Girls vote?

A. They couldn't possibly have anything to do with the Commons.

Why did the Knightsbridge Girl throw away her Gucci belts when the diet failed?

A. Because they were accessories before the fat.

What's the difference between a Knightsbridge Girl and an Essex Girl?

A. Knightsbridge Girls have real jewellery and fake orgasms.

Henrietta: 'I'm 36–24–36.'
Henry: 'I can never remember my bank sort code.'

How long does it take a Knightsbridge Girl to boil an egg?

A. It depends how far she's got on her Cordon Bleu cookery course.

Why did the Knightsbridge Girl fail her driving test?

A. Because she got in the back seat and ordered the examiner to take her home.

How can you tell the bride at a Knightsbridge wedding?

A. She's the one kissing the Labrador.

What is a Knightsbridge Girl's favourite Rolling Stones album?

A. *Get Your Ya-Yas Out!*

What's a Knightsbridge Girl's favourite wine?

A. 'I want to go to Gstaad.'

Why don't Knightsbridge Girls attend gang bangs?

A. They can't bear the thought of all those thank-you letters.

What's the difference between a sheaf of corn and a Knightsbridge Girl?

A. The sheaf of corn has more between the ears.

What's the definition of a Knightsbridge Man?

A. Someone who gets out of the bath to pee.

What's a divorced Knightsbridge Girl's favourite TV programme?

A. *After Henry*.

Why do all Knightsbridge Girls look alike?

A. Beause they're a bunch of inbred-half-witted-parasitical-blood-sucking-sheep-shagging-scumbags-my-name's-Ben-Elton-goodnight.